PRAYER RECIPIES #1

Victory and Healing

Prayer Recipies #1

Victory and Healing

Genevieve Roy

ISBN-978-1-621660-88-0

Published by CSA Publishing
A department of Christian Services Association
P.O. Box 1017, Maricopa, Arizona 85139
www.XPpublishing.com

CSA
PUBLISHING

Contents

PART 3:
SPECIFIC PRAYER WITH BIBLICAL DECLARATION

Part 4:
Healing Prayer with Biblical Declaration

PART 1:

PREPARING FOR VICTORY

The Power of the Tongue

I have had lots of victory in my life by declaring the Word of God. The Bible says:

> For if I pray in a tongue, my spirit prays, but my mind is unfruitful. So what shall I do? I will pray with my spirit, but I will also pray with my understanding; I will sing with my spirit, but I will also sing with my understanding. Otherwise when you are praising God in the Spirit, how can someone else, who is now put in the position of an inquirer, say 'Amen' to your thanksgiving, since they do not know what you are saying? You are giving thanks well enough, but no one else is edified.
>
> — 1 Corinthians 14:14-17 NIV

I have often heard that tongues were intended to help us when we don't know what to pray, but this Scripture tells us that tongues are for our own edification. If we are in a group we can all pray in tongues, but nobody can come in agreement with what we pray unless there is an interpretation. Don't get me wrong here: tongues are important. I have often seen them change the state of someone's mind from desperation to joy. Yet the Scripture we just quoted says that if I pray in tongues, my spirit prays but my mind is unfruitful. It says also that we will pray with understanding. This means that I will either have the interpretation of what I am praying or I will know how to pray.

How can we pray and get results? Does God answer your prayers? I want to help you have more victory in your life of prayer. Do you know that you are called to live in the kingdom while you are still on earth?

> From the days of John the Baptist until now the **kingdom** of heaven **suffers** violence, and the violent take it by force.
>
> — Matthew 11:12

Jesus said, "When you pray, say: 'Our Father in heaven, hallowed be Your name. Your **kingdom come**. Your will be done on **earth** as it is in heaven'" (Luke 11:2).

Why would we pray for the kingdom to come if it could not actually come? Many people pray to go *to* the kingdom and forget to bring it here on earth.

Therefore do not worry, saying, "What shall we eat?" or "What shall we drink?" or "What shall we wear?" For after all these things the Gentiles seek. For your heavenly Father knows that you need all these things. But seek **first** the **kingdom** of God and His righteousness, and all these things shall be added to you.

— Matthew 6:31-33

In the kingdom of God there is no sickness and no lack, so how can we avoid sickness and lack in our lives? Only by faith. "**Without faith** it is impossible to please Him, for he who comes to God must believe that He is, and that He is a rewarder of those who diligently seek Him" (Hebrews 11:5-6).

What is faith? "**Faith is** the **substance** of things hoped for, the evidence of things not seen" (Hebrews 11:1).

To walk in the kingdom, we must believe God and not what we see. Now how can we have the faith when we don't believe? How can we change our mindset to believe? So then **faith comes** by hearing, and hearing by the word of God (see Romans 10:16-18).

What enters into my ears will determine what I believe. If the television is on all day in my house, my faith will come from what I hear from the television. If I declare my Bible and pray using Bible verses, my faith will be built to bring healing and victory in my Christian life. When I speak the Word I also hear the Word, and my faith comes from what I hear. Therefore, I must also be careful of what comes out of my mouth. If I declare the Word of God and then complain to a friend about the situation I just built my faith for, I destroy my prayer of declaration by the negative confession of my mouth.

It is not wrong to talk about your problems to someone, but you must be careful how you do it. You should carefully choose the person with whom you share. Only share with someone who will encourage you and declare the solution with you, using the truth of the gospel. Try not to jump from one person to another to tell your story. Seek comfort in God. If your situation requires many people to pray, ask a prayer group or put it on a prayer chain, but be really careful not to repeat the problem over and over again because what you want is to declare the solution, not the problem.

> Even so, the tongue is a little member and boasts great things. See how great a forest a little fire kindles! Out of the same mouth

proceed blessing and cursing. My brethren, these things ought not to be so. Does a spring send forth fresh water and bitter from the same opening? Can a fig tree, my brethren, bear olives, or a grapevine bear figs? Thus no spring yields both salt water and fresh.

— James 3:5, 10-12

Do not be deceived; God cannot be mocked. A man reaps what he sows. Whoever sows to please their flesh, from the flesh will reap destruction; whoever sows to please the Spirit, from the Spirit will reap eternal life. Let us not become weary in doing good, for at the proper time we will reap a harvest if we do not give up (see Galatians 6:7-9). You will reap what you sow. We know that verse and often use it for financial blessing, but it also applies to the confession of the mouth.

Why do we so often see people do what they said they would never do? As an example, a young girl may confess, "I don't want to be like my mom. She always screams at me, and I will never do that to my child." The girl grows up, has children, and then one day realises that she does exactly the same things that her mother did with her. Why is that? When we judge something, we often become what we judge.

Another example is a loved one, such as husband or wife, who becomes what we always hated in another person, such as our father or mother. That happens because we reap what we sow. If I sow a judgement against someone, I will reap the fruit of that judgement. Forgiveness is the only way out of this vicious cycle. If I speak against someone in my church, I will reap the fruit of what I have spoken against that person. If I complain, I will reap the fruit of it

> A man shall eat well by the fruit of his mouth, but the soul of the unfaithful feeds on violence. He who guards his mouth preserves his life, but he who opens wide his lips shall have destruction.
>
> — Proverbs 13:2-3

When a problem arises, there is a time to speak, but, again, we need to be careful to whom we speak. It's important that we don't go on too long, and we should make sure to pray and declare the truth of the Bible for that situation afterward.

When our daughter Rebecca was in Grade 1 and learning to read, we had a very difficult time because she could not stay focused on what she was doing. She wouldn't sit still to learn; she would forget what she was doing and go do something else. Even in the class, the teachers could not keep her in her seat. She could not remember the letters of the alphabet or read any words. We spent hours trying to teach her how to read. The school sent us to Community Services to determine what was wrong, and she had help every day at school. She took some tests and at the end of that first school year we were told that she had Attention Deficit Disorder and that she would need medication. She still could not read properly.

Because it was the summer, we told them we would wait until the second year. I was thinking, "No way! I rebuke that! There is no way my daughter will have ADD." My husband said, "We must not permit her to have that medication; we will find something else."

I decided to call my friend with whom I pray every week, and I told her about Rebecca's problem. She talked to me about her son and the difficulty they had because of his dyslexia. He was in Grade 8 and could still not tell the difference between a "b" and "d" or a "p" and "q." Like Rebecca, he could not read. My friend and I started declaring the Bible over our children. We used a French book of declaration that uses Bible verses as prayers. We declared whatever prayer came into our hearts from that book.

During the summer before Rebecca started her second grade, I did not make her read very much because she just did not want to do it, and I lacked patience. When she returned to school that year, she was *much* better. During the year, she needed help once a week instead of every day, and she also started to focus on her work at home. Community Services tested her again and told us, "She doesn't have an Attention Deficit Disorder. The problem must be opposition behaviour."

They did not know my God.... My friend and I continued to pray, and by the third year Rebecca no longer needed help. Furthermore, she was in the top three of her class, and she has stayed there ever since. As I write this, she is leading her Grade 9 class.

Also, in the same amount of time, my friend's son was totally healed from dyslexia and he, too, went from the last to the first of his class. The children were at school when we were declaring and praying over them. Rebecca was not aware of her situation and did not know why she had needed help. But even without that knowledge, they have both been healed. Today all my children and I have been healed from asthma, my son and I have been healed by God from a breathing allergy, and my daughter and I have been healed from an allergy to animals. God has given us two dogs, and all of us have learned how to keep our healing. God also healed my knee when the doctor thought I would need an operation. My family and I just go from miracle to miracle. Glory to God!

> Then I heard a loud voice saying in heaven, "Now salvation, and strength, and the kingdom of our God, and the power of His Christ have come, for the accuser of our brethren, who accused them before our God day and night, has been cast down. And they overcame him by the blood of the Lamb and by the word of their testimony, and they did not love their lives to the death. Therefore rejoice, O heavens, and you who dwell in them!"
>
> — Revelation 12:10-12

Some Tips

1. Declare with a loud voice so that you hear it.

So then **faith comes** by hearing, and hearing by the word of God.

— Romans 10:17

So Jesus answered and said to them, "Assuredly, I say to you, if you have faith and do not doubt, you will not only do what was done to the fig tree, but also if you say to this mountain, 'Be removed and be cast into the sea,' it will be done. And whatever things you ask in prayer, **believing**, you will receive."

— Matthew 21:21-22

2. Forgiveness is a choice, not an emotion. If you forgive someone by choice but you feel it is not forgiven in your heart, what do you do? Forgive again with the declaration of your mouth every day until it passes from your brain to your heart.

Then Peter came to Jesus and asked, "Lord, how many times shall I forgive my brother or sister who sins against me? Up to seven times?" Jesus answered, "I tell you, not seven times, but **seventy-seven times**."

— Matthew 18:21-22 NIV

So Jesus answered and said to them, "Have faith in God. For assuredly, I say to you, whoever says to this mountain, 'Be removed and be cast into the sea,' and does not doubt in his heart, but believes that those things he says will be done, he will have whatever he says. Therefore I say to you, whatever things you ask when you pray, believe that you receive them, and you will have them.

— Mark 11:22-24

3. Repeat until you believe; persevere until you have the victory. Some victories come quicly and others take years. It is not about how many times you fail; it is about how many times you will rise up and continue. Paul said:

I have fought the good fight, I have finished the race, I have kept the faith.

— 2 Timothy 4:7

> **Fight** the good **fight** of the **faith**. Take hold
> of the eternal life to which you were called
> when you made your good confession in the
> presence of many witnesses.
>
> — 1 Timothy 6:12 NIV

4. Be careful not to destroy the declaration you make by then complaining about your situation or your difficulties.

> Listen, for I will speak of excellent things,
> and from the opening of my lips will come
> right things; for my mouth will speak truth;
> wickedness is an abomination to my lips. All
> the words of my mouth are with righteousness;
> nothing crooked or perverse is in them.
>
> — Proverbs 8:6-8

5. The more you submit yourself to God and the authority in your life, the more the demons will obey you and the more you will have victory in your life.

> As the Father loved Me, I also have loved
> you; abide in My love. If you keep My
> commandments, you will abide in My love,
> just as I have kept My Father's commandments
> and abide in His love. These things I have
> spoken to you, that My joy may remain in

you, and that your joy may be full. This is My commandment, that you love one another as I have loved you. Greater love has no one than this, than to lay down one's life for his friends. You are My friends if you do whatever I command you. No longer do I call you servants, for a servant does not know what his master is doing; but I have called you friends, for all things that I heard from My Father I have made known to you. You did not choose Me, but I chose you and appointed you that you should go and bear fruit, and that your fruit should remain, that whatever you ask the Father in My name He may give you. These things I command you, that you love one another.

— John 15:9-17

6. If you fall into criticism or complaining, repent, break the curse, declare the truth, and move on.

A good man out of the good treasure of his heart brings forth good; and an evil man out of the evil treasure of his heart brings forth evil. For out of the abundance of the heart his mouth speaks.

— Luke 6:45

7. After you declare, you can also take ten to twenty minutes and soak in that decree. Put on some good music, lie down in a comfortable position, and ask God's presence to change your mindset and cleanse you. Command your thoughts to be captive to the obedience of Christ.

> Be still, and know that I am God; I will be exalted among the nations, I will be exalted in the earth!
>
> – Psalm 46:10

> Be anxious for nothing, but in everything by prayer and supplication, with thanksgiving, let your requests be made known to God; and the peace of God, which surpasses all understanding, will guard your hearts and minds through Christ Jesus. Finally, brethren, whatever things are true, whatever things are noble, whatever things are just, whatever things are pure, whatever things are lovely, whatever things are of good report, if there is any virtue and if there is anything praiseworthy—**meditate on these things**. The things which you learned and received and heard and saw in me, these do, and the God of peace will be with you.
>
> – Philippians 4:6-9

For the weapons of our warfare are not carnal but mighty in God for pulling down strongholds, casting down arguments and every high thing that exalts itself against the knowledge of God, bringing every thought into captivity to the obedience of Christ.

— 2 Corinthians 10:4-5

PART 2:

BIBLICAL DECLARATION

Arise & Shine

I will arise and shine; for my light has come! And the glory of the Lord is risen upon me. For behold, the darkness shall cover the earth, and deep darkness the people; but the Lord will arise over me, and His glory will be seen upon me. The Gentiles shall come to my light, and kings to the brightness of my rising.

I lift up my eyes all around, and see: they all gather together, they come to me; my sons shall come from afar, and my daughters shall be nursed at my side. Then I shall see and become radiant, and my heart shall swell with joy; because the abundance of the sea shall be turned to me, the wealth of the Gentiles shall come to me. The multitude of camels shall cover my land, the dromedaries of Midian and Ephah; all those from Sheba shall come; they shall bring gold and incense, and they shall proclaim the praises of the Lord. All the flocks of Kedar shall be gathered together to me, the rams of Nebaioth shall minister to me; they shall ascend with acceptance on [God's] altar (see Isaiah 60:1-7).

"They shall ascend with acceptance on My altar, and I will glorify the house of My glory. Who are these who fly like a cloud, and like doves to their roosts? Surely the coastlands shall wait for Me; and the ships of Tarshish will come first, to bring your sons from afar, their silver and their gold with them, to the name of the Lord your God, and to the Holy One of Israel, because He has glorified you.

"The sons of foreigners shall build up your walls, and their kings shall minister to you; for in My wrath I struck you, but in My favour I have had mercy on you. Therefore your gates shall be open continually; they shall not be shut day or night, that men may bring to you the wealth of the Gentiles, and their kings in procession. For the nation and kingdom which will not serve you shall perish, and those nations shall be utterly ruined.

"The glory of Lebanon shall come to you, the cypress, the pine, and the box tree together, to beautify the place of My sanctuary; and I will make the place of My feet glorious. Also the sons of those who afflicted you shall come bowing to you, and all those who despised you shall fall prostrate at the soles of your feet; and they shall call you The City of the Lord, Zion of the Holy One of Israel.

"Whereas you have been forsaken and hated, so that no one went through you, I will make you an eternal excellence, a joy of many generations. You shall drink the milk of the Gentiles, and milk the breast of kings; you shall know that I, the Lord, am your Saviour and your Redeemer, the Mighty One of Jacob.

"Instead of bronze I will bring gold, instead of iron I will bring silver, instead of wood, bronze, and instead of stones, iron. I will also make your officers peace, and your magistrates righteousness. Violence shall no longer be heard in your land, neither wasting nor destruction within your borders; but you shall call your walls Salvation, and your gates Praise.

"The sun shall no longer be your light by day, nor for brightness shall the moon give light to you; but the Lord will be to you an everlasting light, and your God your glory. Your sun shall no longer go down, nor shall your moon withdraw itself; for the Lord will be your everlasting light, and the days of your mourning shall be ended. Also your people shall all be righteous; they shall inherit the land forever, the branch of My planting, the work of My hands, that I may be glorified. A little one shall become a thousand, and a small one a strong nation. I, the Lord, will hasten it in its time" (Isaiah 60:7b-22).

The Year of the Lord's Favour

"The Spirit of the Lord God is upon Me, because the Lord has anointed Me to preach good tidings to the poor; He has sent Me to heal the brokenhearted, to proclaim liberty to the captives, and the opening of the prison to those who are bound; to proclaim the acceptable year of the Lord, and the day of vengeance of our God; to comfort all who mourn, to console those who mourn in Zion, to give them beauty for ashes, the oil of joy for mourning, the garment of praise for the spirit of heaviness; that they may be called trees of righteousness, the planting of the Lord, that He may be glorified.

"And they shall rebuild the old ruins, they shall raise up the former desolations, and they shall repair the ruined cities, the desolations of many generations. Strangers shall stand and feed your flocks, and the sons of the foreigner shall be your plowmen and your vinedressers. But you shall be named the priests of the Lord, they shall call you the servants of our God. You shall eat the riches of the Gentiles, and in their glory you shall boast. Instead of your shame you shall have double honour, and instead of confusion they shall rejoice in their portion. Therefore in their land they shall possess double; everlasting joy shall be theirs.

"For I, the Lord, love justice; I hate robbery for burnt offering; I will direct their work in truth, and will make with them an everlasting covenant. Their descendants shall be known among the Gentiles, and their offspring among the people. All who see them shall acknowledge them, that they are the posterity whom the Lord has blessed.

"I will greatly rejoice in the Lord, my soul shall be joyful in my God; for He has clothed me with the garments of salvation, He has covered me with the robe of righteousness, as a bridegroom decks himself with ornaments, and as a bride adorns herself with her jewels. For as the earth brings forth its bud, as the garden causes the things that are sown in it to spring forth, so the Lord God will cause righteousness and praise to spring forth before all the nations" (Isaiah 61).

Zion's New Name

For Zion's sake I will not keep silent, for Jerusalem's sake I will not remain quiet, till her vindication shines out like the dawn, her salvation like a blazing torch. The nations will see our vindication, and all kings our glory; we will be called by a new name that the mouth of the Lord will bestow. We will be a crown of splendour in the Lord's hand, a royal diadem in the hand of our God. No longer will they call us Deserted, or name our land Desolate. But we will be called Hephzibah, and our land Beulah; for the Lord will take delight in us, and our land will be married. As a young man marries a young woman, so will our Builder marry us; as a bridegroom rejoices over his bride, so will our God rejoice over us.

I have posted watchmen on your walls, O Jerusalem; they will never be silent day or night. You who call on the Lord, give yourselves no rest, and give him no rest till he establishes Jerusalem and makes her the praise of the earth.

The Lord has sworn [us] by his right hand and by his mighty arm: "Never again will I give your grain as food for your enemies, and never again will foreigners drink the new wine for which you have toiled; but those who harvest it will eat it and praise the Lord, and those who gather the grapes will drink it in the courts of my sanctuary."

Pass through, pass through the gates! Prepare the way for the people. Build up, build up the highway! Remove the stones. Raise a banner for the nations.

The Lord has made proclamation to the ends of the earth: "Say to Daughter Zion, 'See, your Saviour comes! See, his reward is with him, and his recompense accompanies him.'" [We] will be called the Holy People, the Redeemed of the Lord; and [we] will be called Sought After, the City No Longer Deserted (see Isaiah 62 NIV).

Healing, Victory, & Deliverance

Whoever dwells in the shelter of the Most High will rest in the shadow of the Almighty. I will say of the Lord, "He is my refuge and my fortress, my God, in whom I trust."

Surely he will save [me] from the fowler's snare and from the deadly pestilence. He will cover me with his feathers, and under his wings I will find refuge; his faithfulness will be my shield and rampart. I will not fear the terror of night, nor the arrow that flies by day, nor the pestilence that stalks in the darkness, nor the plague that destroys at midday. A thousand may fall at my side, ten thousand at my right hand, but it will not come near me. I will only observe with my eyes and see the punishment of the wicked.

I declare: The Lord is my refuge, and I make the Most High my dwelling, no harm will overtake me, no disaster will come near my tent. For [God] will command his angels concerning me to guard me in all my ways; they will lift me up in their hands, so that I will not strike my foot against a stone. I will tread on the lion and the cobra; I will trample the great lion and the serpent (see Psalm 91:1-13 NIV).

"'Because he loves me,' says the Lord, 'I will rescue him; I will protect him, for he acknowledges my name. He will call on me, and I will answer him; I will be with him in trouble, I will deliver him and honor him. With long life I will satisfy him and show him my salvation'" (Psalm 91:14-16 NIV).

God Is on Our Side

"Before I formed you in the womb I knew you; before you were born I sanctified you; I ordained you a prophet to the nations" (Jeremiah 1:5).

"'Do not say, "I am too young." You must go to everyone I send you to and say whatever I command you. Do not be afraid of them, for I am with you and will rescue you,' declares the Lord.

"Then the Lord reached out his hand and touched my mouth and said to me, 'I have put my words in your mouth. See, today I appoint you over nations and kingdoms to uproot and tear down, to destroy and overthrow, to build and to plant'" (Jeremiah 7-10 NIV).

We trust in the Lord, and we do good; we dwell in the land and enjoy safe pasture. We take delight in the Lord, and He will give us the desires of our heart. Because we commit our way to the Lord and we trust in Him, He will do this: He will make our righteous reward shine like the dawn, our vindication like the noonday sun (see Psalm 37:3-6 NIV).

May the Lord answer us when we are in distress; may the name of the God of Jacob protect us. May he send us help from the sanctuary and grant us support from Zion. May he remember all our sacrifices and accept our burnt offerings. May he give us the desire of our heart and make all our plans succeed. May we shout for joy over our victory and lift up our banners in the name of our God. May the Lord grant all our requests.

Now this I know: the Lord gives victory to his anointed. He answers him from his heavenly sanctuary with the victorious power of his right hand. Some trust in chariots and some in horses, but we trust in the name of the Lord our God. They are brought to their knees and fall, but we rise up and stand firm. Lord, give victory to the king! Answer us when we call (see Psalm 20 NIV).

Declaring God's
Glory & Kingdom

"My heart is overflowing with a good theme; I recite my composition concerning the King; my tongue is the pen of a ready writer.

"You are fairer than the sons of men; grace is poured upon Your lips; therefore God has blessed You forever. Gird Your sword upon Your thigh, O Mighty One, with Your glory and Your majesty. And in Your majesty ride prosperously because of truth, humility, and righteousness; and Your right hand shall teach You awesome things. Your arrows are sharp in the heart of the King's enemies; the peoples fall under You.

"Your throne, O God, is forever and ever; a sceptre of righteousness is the sceptre of Your kingdom. You love righteousness and hate wickedness; therefore God, Your God, has anointed You with the oil of gladness more than Your companions. All Your garments are scented with myrrh and aloes and cassia, out of the ivory palaces, by which they have made You glad. Kings' daughters are among Your honourable women; at Your right hand stands the queen in gold from Ophir.

"Listen, O daughter, consider and incline your ear; forget your own people also, and your father's house; so the King will greatly desire your beauty; because He is your Lord, worship Him. And the daughter of Tyre will come with a gift; the rich among the people will seek your favour.

"The royal daughter is all glorious within the palace; Her clothing is woven with gold. She shall be brought to the King in robes of many colours; the virgins, her companions who follow her, shall be brought to You. With gladness and rejoicing they shall be brought; they shall enter the King's palace.

"Instead of Your fathers shall be Your sons, whom You shall make princes in all the earth. I will make Your name to be remembered in all generations; therefore the people shall praise You forever and ever" (Psalm 45).

Victory & Joy

Because we have the blood of Jesus we declare:

Let our flesh be renewed like a child's; let us be restored as in the days of our youth — then we can pray to God and find favour with him, we will see God's face and shout for joy; he will restore us to full well-being. And we will go to others and say, "I have sinned. I have perverted what is right, but I did not get what I deserved. God has delivered me from going down to the pit, and I shall live to enjoy the light of life."

God does all these things to people — twice, even three times — to turn them back from the pit, that the light of life may shine on them.

I will pay attention and listen to God; I will be silent and he will speak, [because God said,] "Be silent, and I will teach you wisdom" (see Job 33:25-31,33 NIV).

"'Sing, O barren, you who have not borne! Break forth into singing, and cry aloud, you who have not laboured with child! For more are the children of the desolate than the children of the married woman,' says the Lord. 'Enlarge the place of your tent, and let them stretch out the curtains of your dwellings; do not spare; lengthen your cords, and strengthen your stakes. For you shall expand to the right and to the left, and your descendants will inherit the nations, and make the desolate cities inhabited.

"'Do not fear, for you will not be ashamed; neither be disgraced, for you will not be put to shame; for you will forget the shame of your youth, and will not remember the reproach of your widowhood anymore. For your Maker is your husband, the Lord of hosts is His name; and your Redeemer is the Holy One of Israel; He is called the God of the whole earth. For the Lord has called you like a woman forsaken and grieved in spirit, like a youthful wife when you were refused,' says your God. 'For a mere moment I have forsaken you, but with great mercies I will gather you. With a little wrath I hid My face from you for a moment; but with everlasting kindness I will have mercy on you,' says the Lord, your Redeemer.

"'For this is like the waters of Noah to Me; for as I have sworn that the waters of Noah would no longer cover the earth, so have I sworn that I would not be angry with you, nor rebuke you. For the mountains shall depart and the hills be removed, but My kindness shall not depart from you, nor shall My covenant of peace be removed,' says the Lord, who has mercy on you.

"'O you afflicted one, tossed with tempest, and not comforted, behold, I will lay your stones with colourful gems, and lay your foundations with sapphires. I will make your pinnacles of rubies, your gates of crystal, and all your walls of precious stones. All your children shall be taught by the Lord, and great shall be the peace of your children. In righteousness you shall be established; you shall be far from oppression, for you shall not fear; and from terror, for it shall not come near you. Indeed they shall surely assemble, but not because of Me. Whoever assembles against you shall fall for your sake.

"'Behold, I have created the blacksmith who blows the coals in the fire, who brings forth an instrument for his work; and I have created the spoiler to destroy. No weapon formed against you shall prosper, and every tongue which rises against you in judgement you shall condemn. This is the heritage of the servants of the Lord, and their righteousness is from Me,' says the Lord" (Isaiah 54).

REDEMPTION IN CHRIST

"Grace to you and peace from God our Father and the Lord Jesus Christ.

"Blessed be the God and Father of our Lord Jesus Christ, who has blessed us with every spiritual blessing in the heavenly places in Christ, just as He chose us in Him before the foundation of the world, that we should be holy and without blame before Him in love, having predestined us to adoption as sons by Jesus Christ to Himself, according to the good pleasure of His will, to the praise of the glory of His grace, by which He made us accepted in the Beloved.

"In Him we have redemption through His blood, the forgiveness of sins, according to the riches of His grace which He made to abound toward us in all wisdom and prudence, having made known to us the mystery of His will, according to His good pleasure which He purposed in Himself, that in the dispensation of the fullness of the times He might gather together in one all things in Christ, both which are in heaven and which are on earth — in Him. In Him also we have obtained an inheritance, being predestined according to the purpose of Him who works all things according to the counsel of His will, that we who first trusted in Christ should be to the praise of His glory.

"In Him you also trusted, after you heard the word of truth, the gospel of your salvation; in whom also, having believed, you were sealed with the Holy Spirit of promise, who is the guarantee of our inheritance until the redemption of the purchased possession, to the praise of His glory" (Ephesians 1:2-14).

Prayer for Spiritual Wisdom

Father God, according to Ephesians 1:17-23, we pray that You, the God of our Lord Jesus Christ, the Father of glory, may give to us the spirit of wisdom and revelation in the knowledge of You, the eyes of our understanding being enlightened; that we may know what is the hope of Your calling, what are the riches of the glory of Your inheritance in the saints, and what is the exceeding greatness of Your power toward us who believe, according to the working of Your mighty power which You worked in Christ when You raised Him from the dead and seated Him at Your right hand in the heavenly places, far above all principality and power and might and dominion, and every name that is named, not only in this age but also in that which is to come.

And You put all things under His feet, and gave Him to be head over all things to the church, which is His body, the fullness of You who fills all in all" (see Ephesians 1:17-23).

GRACE THROUGH FAITH

Thank You, Father God, for being "rich in mercy, because of Your great love with which You loved us, even when we were dead in trespasses, made us alive together with Christ (by Your grace we have been saved), and raised us up together, and made us sit together in the heavenly places in Christ Jesus, that in the ages to come You might show the exceeding riches of Your grace in Your kindness toward us in Christ Jesus. For by grace we have been saved through faith, and that not of ourselves; it is the gift of God, not of works, lest anyone should boast. For we are Your workmanship, created in Christ Jesus for good works, which You, Father God, prepared beforehand that we should walk in them (see Ephesians 2:4-10).

But now in Christ Jesus we who once were far off have been brought near by the blood of Christ. For Christ Himself is our peace, who has made both one, and has broken down the middle wall of separation, having abolished in His flesh the enmity, that is, the law of commandments contained in ordinances, so as to create in Himself one new man from the two, thus making peace, and that He might reconcile them both to God in one body through the cross, thereby putting to death the enmity. And He came and preached peace to [us] who were afar off and to those who were near. For through Him we both have access by one Spirit to the Father.

Now, therefore, we are no longer strangers and foreigners, but fellow citizens with the saints and members of the household of God, having been built on the foundation of the apostles and prophets, Jesus Christ Himself being the chief cornerstone, in whom the whole building, being fitted together, grows into a holy temple in the Lord, in whom we also are being built together for a dwelling place of God in the Spirit (see Ephesians 2:13-22).

Appreciation of the Mystery

We bow our knees to the Father of our Lord Jesus Christ, from whom the whole family in heaven and earth is named, that He would grant us, according to the riches of His glory, to be strengthened with might through His Spirit in our inner man, that Christ may dwell in our hearts through faith; that we, being rooted and grounded in love, may be able to comprehend with all the saints what is the width and length and depth and height — to know the love of Christ which passes knowledge; that we may be filled with all the fullness of God.

Now to Him who is able to do exceedingly abundantly above all that we ask or think, according to the power that works in us, to Him be glory in the church by Christ Jesus to all generations, forever and ever. Amen (see Ephesians 3:14-21).

Walk in Unity

for Spiritual Gifts

Lord, we want to walk worthy of the calling with which we were called, with all lowliness and gentleness, with longsuffering, bearing with one another in love, endeavouring to keep the unity of the Spirit in the bond of peace. There is one body and one Spirit, just as we were called in one hope of our calling; one Lord, one faith, one baptism; one God and Father of all, who is above all, and through all, and in us all. To each one of us grace was given according to the measure of Christ's gift.

"Therefore He says: 'When He ascended on high, He led captivity captive, and gave gifts to men.' (Now this, 'He ascended' — what does it mean but that He also first descended into the lower parts of the earth? He who descended is also the One who ascended far above all the heavens, that He might fill all things.) And He Himself gave some to be apostles, some prophets, some evangelists, and some pastors and teachers, for the equipping of the saints for the work of ministry, for the edifying of the body of Christ, till we all come to the unity of the faith and of the knowledge of the Son of God, to a perfect man, to the measure of the stature of the fullness of Christ; that we should no longer be children, tossed to and fro and carried about with every wind of doctrine, by the trickery of men, in the cunning craftiness of deceitful plotting, but, speaking the truth in love, may grow up in all things into Him who is the head – Christ – from whom the whole body, joined and knit together by what every joint supplies, according to the effective working by which every part does its share, causes growth of the body for the edifying of itself in love" (see Ephesians 4:1-8, 8-16).

So we choose to no longer walk as the rest of the Gentiles walk...

Do Not Grieve the Spirit

Be renewed in the spirit of our mind, and put on the new man which was created according to God, in true righteousness and holiness.

Therefore, putting away lying, "Let each one of us speak truth with our neighbour," for we are members of one another. We won't let the sun go down on our wrath, nor give place to the devil. We will let him who stole steal no longer, but rather we will require him to labour, working with his hands what is good, that he may have something to give him who has need. We will let no corrupt word proceed out of our mouth, but what is good for necessary edification, that it may impart grace to the hearers. And we will not grieve the Holy Spirit of God, by whom we were sealed for the day of redemption. We will let all bitterness, wrath, anger, clamour, and evil speaking be put away from us, with all malice, so that we can be kind to one another, tenderhearted, forgiving one another, even as God in Christ forgave us (see Ephesians 4:23-32).

Walk in Love, Light, & Wisdom

Father, help us to be imitators of God as dear children. And help us to walk in love, as Christ also has loved us and given Himself for us, an offering and a sacrifice to God for a sweet-smelling aroma (see Ephesians 5:1-2).

For we were once darkness, but now we are light in the Lord. We want to walk as children of light and with the fruit of the Spirit that is in all goodness, righteousness, and truth, finding out what is acceptable to the Lord. Give us discernment so that we will have no fellowship with the unfruitful works of darkness, but rather expose them. We declare that all things that are exposed are made manifest by the light, for whatever makes manifest is light. Therefore we declare with You: "Awake, you who sleep, arise from the dead, and Christ will give you light."

We choose to walk circumspectly, not as fools but as wise, redeeming the time, because the days are evil. Therefore Father, help us not be unwise, but understand what Your will is. We choose to not be drunk with wine, in which is dissipation; but be filled with the Spirit, speaking to one another in psalms and hymns and spiritual songs, singing and making melody in our heart to the Lord, giving thanks always for all things to You Father in the name of our Lord Jesus Christ, submitting to one another in the fear of You God (see Ephesians 5:8-21).

Marks of the Ministry

We then, as workers together with Him, do not receive the grace of God in vain (see 2 Corinthians 6:1).

"For He says: 'In an acceptable time I have heard you, and in the day of salvation I have helped you.' Behold, now is the accepted time; behold, now is the day of salvation.

"We give no offense in anything, that our ministry may not be blamed. But in all things we commend ourselves as ministers of God: in much patience, in tribulations, in needs, in distresses, in stripes, in imprisonment, in tumults, in labours, in sleeplessness, in fastings; by purity, by knowledge, by longsuffering, by kindness, by the Holy Spirit, by sincere love, by the word of truth, by the power of God, by the armour of righteousness on the right hand and on the left, by honour and dishonour, by evil report and good report; as deceivers, and yet true; as unknown, and yet well known; as dying, and behold we live; as chastened, and yet not killed; as sorrowful, yet always rejoicing; as poor, yet making many rich; as having nothing, and yet possessing all things" (2 Corinthians 6:2-10).

Be Holy

For we are the temple of the living God.

As God has said: "I will dwell in them and walk among them. I will be their God, and they shall be My people." Therefore "Come out from among them and be separate," says the Lord. "Do not touch what is unclean, and I will receive you. I will be a Father to you, and you shall be My sons and daughters," says the Lord Almighty (see 2 Corinthians 6:16-18).

Some Warrior Verses

"The Lord has heard my supplication; the Lord will receive my prayer. Let all my enemies be ashamed and greatly troubled; let them turn back and be ashamed suddenly" (Psalm 6:9-10).

"When the enemy comes in like a flood, the Spirit of the Lord will lift up a standard against him" (Isaiah 59:19).

"I have pursued my enemies and overtaken them; neither did I turn back again till they were destroyed. I have wounded them, so that they could not rise; they have fallen under my feet. For You have armed me with strength for the battle; You have subdued under me those who rose up against me. You have also given me the necks of my enemies, so that I destroyed those who hated me. They cried out, but there was none to save; even to the Lord, but He did not answer them. Then I beat them as fine as the dust before the wind; I cast them out like dirt in the streets.

"You have delivered me from the strivings of the people; You have made me the head of the nations; a people I have not known shall serve me. As soon as they hear of me they obey me; the foreigners submit to me. The foreigners fade away, and come frightened from their hideouts" (Psalm 18:37-45).

"Oh, clap your hands, all you peoples! Shout to God with the voice of triumph! For the Lord Most High is awesome; He is a great King over all the earth. He will subdue the peoples under us, and the nations under our feet. He will choose our inheritance for us, the excellence of Jacob whom He loves" (Psalm 47:1-4).

"Therefore God also has highly exalted Him [Jesus] and given Him the name which is above every name, that at the name of Jesus every knee should bow, of those in heaven, and of those on earth, and of those under the earth, and that every tongue should confess that Jesus Christ is Lord, to the glory of God the Father" (Philippians 2:9-11).

"And you, being dead in your trespasses and the uncircumcision of your flesh, He has made alive together with Him [Jesus], having forgiven you all trespasses, having wiped out the handwriting of requirements that was against us, which was contrary to us.

And He has taken it out of the way, having nailed it to the cross. Having disarmed principalities and powers, He made a public spectacle of them, triumphing over them in it" (Colossians 2:13-15).

And we know that for those who love God, that is, for those who are called according to his purpose, all things are working together for good (see Romans 8:28).

Part 3:

Specific Prayer
with Biblical Declaration

Declaration for a Loved One

or a Backslider

For more information, see teaching on blood and soul connections.

I speak to the soul of _____ (name of the person).

I declare that _____ is a lover of God who seeks first the kingdom of God and His righteousness (see Matthew 6:33).

I declare that _____ forgives anything against anyone so that our Father in heaven may also forgive them their trespasses (see Mark 11:25).

I declare that _____ abides in the Word of God and seeks the truth, which is Jesus, and the truth will set him/her free. Jesus will make _____ free and they will be free indeed (see John 8:32,36).

I declare that _____ is a good soldier of Jesus Christ. They do not become entangled with the affairs of this life so that they may please Jesus who enlisted _____ as a soldier (see 2 Timothy 2:3-4).

Because of His great love, God, who is rich in mercy, loved _____ even when they were dead in trespasses. God has made them alive with Christ. By grace _____ has been saved, and God has raised them up to sit in the heavenly places in Christ Jesus, that in the ages to come He might show the exceeding riches of His grace in His kindness toward _____ (see Ephesians 2:4-7).

I declare that _____ puts on the helmet of salvation—the salvation through the blood of Jesus—and that it would be on _____'s head like a filter to discern truth from everything that is seen or heard so _____ will have the wisdom and knowledge to keep their thoughts captive to the obedience of Christ.

Prayer for Wisdom with an Unsaved Person

Lord please forgive me for every time my life has not been a testimony for _____ and every time I did not love _____ like Christ. Forgive me for every judgement or curse I have pronounced or thought against _____. I break the power of those curses now in the name of Jesus.

Now I declare that the Spirit of the Lord God is upon Me, because the Lord has anointed Me to preach good tidings to _____ (see Isaiah 61:1). Lord, give me words for _____ and the wisdom to know when to speak to him/her. Lord, I believe that You have sent me into the life of _____ to bring healing to their broken heart. I proclaim liberty to _____, and the opening of the prison for _____, because he/she is bound; I proclaim the acceptable year of the Lord in _____'s life, so that Jesus will be recognised as _____ Saviour and won't be touched by the day of vengeance of our God because Jesus will set _____ free. Lord, give me the words _____ needs to hear so that You can comfort them. You give _____ beauty for ashes, the oil of joy for mourning, the garment of praise for the spirit of heaviness; that they may be called a tree of righteousness, the planting of the Lord, that You may be glorified (inspired by Isaiah 61:1).

Prayer for a Loved One from Our Father's Prayer

Father, thank You that You are already working in the life of _____. Bless them in their life.

Our Father in heaven, hallowed be Your name in the life of _____. May Your kingdom come and Your will be done in their life on earth as it is in heaven. Give them this day their daily bread so they will be nurtured and fed in the truth of Your gospel and grow in Your wisdom. Forgive _____'s debts as You teach them, and give them the grace to forgive their debtors. Do not lead _____ into temptation, but deliver them from the evil one. Give _____ discernment so they won't be seduced by the enemy's plan. For Yours is the kingdom and the power and the glory forever!

Give _____ the grace to be a good ground and yield a crop of a hundredfold (see Matthew 6:9-13 & 13:8).

Prayer for a Husband

(from his wife)

Father God, first I want to ask Your forgiveness.

Please forgive me for every time I judged my husband. Forgive me for every criticism and every time I have spoken against him. Forgive me for every time I have cursed him; I break the power of those curses now, in the name of Jesus. *(Ask God if there are things for which you need to forgive your husband.)*

I choose to be careful with my words and use my tongue to bless, not to curse. I choose to honour my husband with what I do and what I say.

Now, in the name of Jesus, I declare and speak to the soul of _____ (his name), that he is a man of faith who seeks first the kingdom of God and His righteousness (see Matthew 6:33).

I declare that my husband shall put on the helmet of salvation, through the blood of Jesus, so that it shall be on his head like a filter of the truth to discern everything he sees and hears, so he will have the wisdom and knowledge to keep his thoughts captive to the obedience of Christ.

I declare that my husband abides in the Word of God. He seeks the truth, which is Jesus, and the truth will set him free. Jesus will make _____ free, and he will be free indeed! I declare that my husband is a friend of Jesus and does whatever God commands him to do. He is no longer a servant, because he seeks to know Jesus. Jesus chose and appointed _____ so that he would bear fruit that remains, and whatever he will ask the Father in the name of Jesus, the Father will give him. I declare my husband is an instrument of love in the hand of the Father (see John 8:32,36 & 15:14-17).

I declare that he does not turn to the right or to the left from any of the words which God has commanded us in the Bible. He won't go after other gods to serve them (see Deuteronomy 28:14).

I declare that as a couple, my husband and I are holy. We act with tender mercy, kindness, humility, meekness, and longsuffering; we bear with one another and forgive one another as Christ has forgiven us. Above all things, we act with love, which is the bond of perfection. And we choose to let the peace of God rule in our hearts.

I declare that the Word of Christ will richly dwell in us with all wisdom. We will teach and admonish one another in psalms, hymns, and spiritual songs, singing with grace in our hearts to the Lord. I pray this in the name of the Lord Jesus, and we give glory to God the Father through Him.

I choose to submit to my husband, as is fitting in the Lord. I declare that my husband loves me and he is not bitter toward me (see Colossians 3:12-13, 15-19).

I declare that the heart of my husband safely trusts me, so that he will have no lack of gain. And I choose to do him good and not evil all the days of my life. My husband praises and encourages me because I fear the Lord (see Proverbs 31:11-12,28).

Prayer for a Wife

(from her Husband)

Father God, first I want to ask Your forgiveness. Please forgive me for every time I have judged my wife. Forgive me for every criticism and every time I have spoken against her. Forgive me for every time I have cursed her; I break the power of those curses now, in the name of Jesus. I choose to be careful with my words and use my tongue to bless, not to curse. *(Ask God if there are things for which you need to forgive your wife.)*

I choose to honour my wife with my actions and with my mouth. I declare that from now on, I will praise her (see Proverbs 31:28).

Now, in the name of Jesus, I declare and speak to the soul of _____ (her name), that she is a woman of faith who seeks first the kingdom of God and His righteousness (see Matthew 6:33).

I declare that my wife shall put on the helmet of salvation, through the blood of Jesus, so that it shall be on her head like a filter of the truth to discern everything she sees and hears so she will have the wisdom and knowledge to keep her thoughts captive to the obedience of Christ.

I declare that my wife abides in the Word of God. She seeks the truth, which is Jesus, and the truth sets her free. Jesus will make _____ free, and she will be free indeed! I declare that my wife is a friend of Jesus and does whatever God commands her to do. She is no longer a servant, because she seeks to know Jesus. Jesus chose and appointed _____ so that she will go and bear fruit, and that her fruit remains, so that whatever she will ask the Father in the name of Jesus, the Father will give her. I declare my wife is an instrument of love in the hand of the Father (see John 8:32,36 & 15:14-17).

I declare that she does not turn to the right or the left from any of the Words which God has commanded us in the Bible. She won't go after other gods to serve them (see Deuteronomy 28:14).

I declare that as a couple, my wife and I are holy. We act with tender mercy, kindness, humility, meekness, and longsuffering; we bear with one another and forgive one another as Christ has forgiven us. Above all things, we act with love, which is the bond of perfection. And we choose to let the peace of God rule in our hearts.

I declare that we let the Word of Christ richly dwell in us with all wisdom. We will teach and admonish one another in psalms, hymns, and spiritual songs, singing with grace in our hearts to the Lord. I pray this in the name of the Lord Jesus, and we give glory to God the Father through Him.

I choose to submit to the Lord Jesus and to lead and serve my household and my wife with righteousness and wisdom in obedience to the Word of God. I declare that my wife loves me and she is not bitter toward me (see Colossians 3:12-13, 15-19).

Lord, please forgive me for every time I did not trust or believe my wife. I declare that my wife is a virtuous woman and her worth is far above rubies. Because of that, my heart safely trusts her; I will have no lack of gain. My wife does me good and not evil all the days of her life.

I declare that all she touches brings forth prosperity in our home. Many wives have done well, but my wife exceeds them all, because she fears the Lord (see Proverbs 31:10-12, 29-30).

Prayer for a Teen or Child

Teens can also use this prayer to pray for their future husband or wife. If it is not your own child, do the forgiveness part for the child's parents.

Lord, I ask You to forgive me for every time I provoked _____ (child's name) to anger and every time I discourage them.

I declare that _____ follows God's commands and obeys their parents and authority, as God gives their parents and those in authority the wisdom to raise them in the truth of the Bible. I declare that _____ honours their parents and authority in all good things, for this is well pleasing to the Lord, that _____ may be well in God and live long on the earth (see Ephesians 6:1-4, Colossians 3:20-21).

I declare that _____ continues in the things they have learned from the Word of God and that from childhood _____ will know the Holy Scriptures, which are able to make them wise for salvation through faith, which is in Christ Jesus. _____ seeks the truth, which is Jesus, and the truth sets them free. Jesus will make _____ free and they will be free indeed (see John 8:31-32,36)!

_____ is a man/woman of faith who seeks first the kingdom of God and His righteousness (see Matthew 6:33).

Thank You, Lord, that You give _____ the will, ability, and knowledge to be fruitful at school and with their homework. Help them in everything they do, and give them the capacity to keep their thoughts captive to the obedience of Christ.

So _____ is a vessel of honour because he/ she cleans himself/herself in the blood of Jesus. They are sanctified and useful for the Master, ready to do every good work that the Lord sets before them. _____ also flees youthful lusts and pursues righteousness, faith, love, and peace with those who call on the Lord out of a pure heart. _____ avoids foolish and ignorant disputes, knowing that they generate strife. _____ is a good servant of the Lord who does not quarrel, but is gentle to all, able to teach and be patient. In humility, they correct those who are in opposition, so that God perhaps will grant them repentance, that they may know the truth (see 2 Timothy 2:20-25).

_____ preaches the Word! They are ready in season and out of season to convince, rebuke, and exhort with all longsuffering and teaching. _____ is watchful in all things, endures afflictions, does the work of an evangelist, and fulfills their ministry. They will fight the good fight and keep the faith until the race is finished (see 2 Timothy 4:2,5,7).

_____ lets no one despise their youth, but is an example to the believers in word, in conduct, in love, in spirit, in faith, and in purity (see 1 Timothy 4:12). God gives _____ strength and wisdom to keep himself/herself for the husband/wife that God has for them.

_____ flees the love of money and pursues righteousness, godliness, faith, love, patience and gentleness. _____ obeys the commandment of the Lord and keeps himself/herself without spot, blameless until our Lord Jesus Christ's appearing (see 1 Timothy 6:11-14).

Thank You, Lord, for _____'s life and for what You are doing in them. Thank You that they fear God, not man.

Lord, You pour out Your Spirit on _____ so that they shall prophesy, see visions, and have dreams. Give _____ discernment, wisdom and interpretation of all they receive from You. _____ will see wonders in heaven above and signs in the earth beneath before the coming of the great and awesome day of the Lord. And it shall come to pass that whoever calls on the name of the Lord shall be saved (see Acts 2:17-21).

Prayer Against

Discouragement

Father God, I ask You to forgive me for being discouraged. I choose to forgive any person who has hurt me or that the enemy has used against me in my life (name them if needed).

According to 2 Corinthian 4:8-10, I declare that though I am hard-pressed on every side, I am not crushed. I am perplexed but not in despair, persecuted but not abandoned, struck down but not destroyed. I always carry in my body the death of Jesus so the life of Jesus may also manifest in my body (NKJV combined with NIV).

Father God, You are faithful. You will not allow me to be tempted beyond what I am able to bear, but with the temptation, You will also make the way of escape (see 1 Corinthians 10:13).

Lord, You came to earth to console those who mourn, to give them beauty for ashes, the oil of joy for mourning, and the garment of praise for the spirit of heaviness so we may be called trees of righteousness, the planting of the Lord, that You may be glorified (see Isaiah 61:3).

Your Word says that the weapons of our warfare are not carnal but mighty in God for pulling down strongholds, casting down arguments and every high thing that exalts itself against the knowledge of God. Knowing that, I command my thoughts to be brought into captivity to the obedience of Christ (see 2 Corinthians 10:4-5).

I choose to praise You and be grateful to You.

"Bless the Lord, O my soul, and all that is within me, bless His holy name! Bless the Lord, O my soul, and forget not all His benefits: Who forgives all your iniquities, Who heals all your diseases, Who redeems your life from destruction, Who crowns you with lovingkindness and tender mercies, Who satisfies your mouth with good things, so that your youth is renewed like the eagle's" (Psalm 103:1-5).

"Return to your rest, O my soul, for the Lord has dealt bountifully with you" (Psalm 116:7).

I declare that in this situation (name it) God works for my good because I love Him and I have been called according to His purpose (see Romans 8:28).

Lord, help me remember Your goodness toward me. I choose to put my trust in You for every situation in my life. I choose not worry, for my heavenly Father knows all that I need. I will seek **first** the **kingdom** of God and His righteousness, and all these things shall be added to me (see Matthew 6:31-34).

I choose to rest in You, and I give You every burden (name them) in my life. I choose to be anxious for nothing, but in everything by prayer and supplication with thanksgiving, I will let my requests be made known to God; and the peace of God, which surpasses all understanding, will guard my heart and mind through Christ Jesus (see Philippians 4:4-7).

Continue with worship music, thanksgiving, or victory declarations. You can also use, according to your situation, my prayer called "Claiming your Blessing for Prosperity".

"Come to Me, all you who labour and are heavy laden, and I will give you rest. Take My yoke upon you and learn from Me, for I am gentle and lowly in heart, and you will find rest for your souls. For My yoke is easy and My burden is light" (Matthew 11:28-30).

Rebuking Anger

Father God, I recognise that the anger I feel is a form of fear and control. I ask You to forgive my fear and my lack of trust in You. Forgive me for trying to control this situation in my life (name it), or any other situation, by using anger. I choose to put my trust in You. I ask You for forgiveness for any curse that I have spoken through anger against me and against others. I break the impact of those curses now, in the name of Jesus.

I renounce anger, fear, control, irritation, and self-justification. I choose to be careful with my words and use my tongue to bless, not to curse. *Ask God if there is anyone you need to forgive, and forgive them.*

According to Proverbs 18:21, "Death and life are in the power of the tongue, and those who love it will eat its fruit."

Lord, give me the tongue of the learned so I will know how to speak a word in season to anyone who is weary (see Isaiah 50:4).

Lord, help me to be slow to anger, that my glory be to overlook a transgression (see Proverbs 19:11).

"[I] do not wrestle against flesh and blood, but against principalities, against powers, against the rulers of the darkness of this age, against spiritual hosts of wickedness in the heavenly places" (Ephesians 6:12).

I choose to fight the good fight of faith and lay hold of eternal life (see 1 Timothy 6:12).

Rebuking Tiredness

If tiredness comes from a sickness, see "General Healing" or Psalm 91.

Lord Jesus, I ask You to forgive me for every time I did not wait upon You, every time I worried, and every burden I took on my shoulders.

Lord, I come to You with my heavy burden so that You can give me rest. I want to give You my yoke as I take Your yoke and learn from You, because You are gentle and lowly in heart, and I will find rest for my soul in You. Your yoke is easy and Your burden is light (see Matthew 11:28-30).

I renounce and rebuke any form of tiredness, in the name of Jesus. I choose not to worry because You, my heavenly Father, know everything I need and everything I am going through. I choose to seek first the kingdom of God and His righteousness, and all the things I need will be added to me (see Matthew 6:31-34).

I choose to wait on You so that You will renew my strength; I declare that I will mount up with wings like an eagle; I will run and not be weary; I will walk and not faint (see Isaiah 40:31).

"I will both lie down in peace and sleep; for You alone, O Lord, make me dwell in safety" (Psalm 4:8-9).

I declare that my inward man is being renewed day by day (see 2 Corinthians 4:16).

Thank You, Lord, that You make me to lie down in green pastures; You lead me beside the still waters, and You restore my soul; You lead me in the paths of righteousness for Your name's sake. You prepare a table before me in the presence of my enemies; You anoint my head with oil, and my cup runs over. Surely, goodness and mercy shall follow me all the days of my life, and I will dwell in the house of the Lord forever (see Psalm 23:2-3, 5-6).

CLAIMING YOUR BLESSING

FOR PROSPERITY

Lord, I ask You to forgive me for every time I disobeyed You in my life and every time I did not give You my offering with gladness or robbed You by not giving it. I recognise that I have not consulted You while trying to rule my own finances. Please forgive me.

Now I choose to obey the voice of the Lord my God and to observe carefully all His commandments. Because I repent of my sins, I am also justified by the blood of Jesus Christ so that the Lord my God will set me high above all nations of the earth. All these blessings are coming upon me and they overtake me because I obey the voice of the Lord my God. I am blessed in the city, and I am blessed in the country. The fruit of my body is blessed; the produce of my ground and the increase of my herds, the increase of my cattle and the offspring of my flocks are blessed. My basket and my kneading bowl are blessed. I am blessed coming in and blessed when I go out. The Lord will cause my enemies who rise against me to be defeated before my face. When they come out against me one way, they will flee before me seven ways. The Lord has commanded a blessing on me in my storehouses and in all to which I set my hand, and He will bless me in the land, which the Lord my God has given me. The Lord is establishing me as a holy person to Himself just as He has sworn to me. If I keep the commandments of the Lord my God and walk in His ways, then all peoples of the earth will see that I am called by the name of the Lord, and they will be afraid of me. The Lord is granting me plenty of goods in the fruit of my body, in the increase of my livestock, and in the produce of my ground in the land that the Lord swore to my fathers to give me. The Lord is opening to me His good treasure, the heavens, to give rain to my land in its season and to bless all the work of my hands. I will lend to many nations but will not borrow. And the Lord has made me the head and not the tail; I will be above only and not beneath, because I heed the commandments of the Lord my God and am careful to observe them. I will not turn aside from any of the words that God commands me this day. I will not turn to the right or the left to go after other gods to serve them (see Deuteronomy 28:1-14).

That means that I lack nothing. The work of my hands (my business) is blessed, and God gives me strategies to increase my income. It also means that I have so much food that I can give to the needy. It means that all my bills are paid, my credit cards are paid, my debts are paid, and I can help others to pay their bills. It is done. Jesus has disarmed the powers and authorities. He made a public spectacle of them, triumphing over them by the cross (see Colossians 2:15).

See also "True Identity" and "Declaring Financial Breakthrough".

DECLARING FINANCIAL

BREAKTHROUGH

Lord, I ask Your forgiveness for every time I did not obey You in my tithes and offerings and for sowing sparingly (see 2 Corinthians 9:6-8).

Forgive me for longing for things that my neighbours, family, and friends have. Forgive me for listening to my fear and emotion instead of putting my trust in You. I ask Your forgiveness for my fear of lack and poverty-mentality. I command my thoughts to be in captivity to the obedience of Christ (see 2 Corinthians 10:5).

Ask God if there is someone you need to forgive.

Lord, I choose now to take on a kingdom-mentality and believe for Your kingdom to come and Your will be done in my life as it is in heaven. I lack nothing because You give me my daily bread (see Matthew 6:10-11).

I believe that I sow bountifully and I will also reap bountifully. I give as I purpose with joy in my heart, for God loves a cheerful giver. God is making all grace abound toward me so that I always have all sufficiency in all things, and I may have an abundance for every good work. Not only that, but God is the One who supplies seed to me and bread for food. He supplies and multiplies the seed I have sown and increases the fruits of my righteousness. I am enriched in everything for all liberality, and this causes me to give thanks to God (see 2 Corinthians 9:6-8, 10-11).

"My God shall supply all [my] need according to His riches in glory by Christ Jesus" (Philippians 4:19).

God will open for me the windows of heaven and pour out for me such blessing that there will not be room enough to receive it. He will rebuke the devourer for my sake so that he will not destroy the fruit of my ground, nor shall the vine fail to bear fruit for me in the field. All nations will call me blessed, for I will be as a delightful land (see Malachi 3:10-12).

Thank You, Lord, that because I give, it will be given to me in good measure, pressed down, shaken together, and running over will be put into my bosom. When I give, please give me wisdom to know which measure I should give, because with the same measure that I use, it will be measured back to me (see Luke 6:38).

"The Lord rewarded me according to my righteousness; according to the cleanness of my hands He has recompensed me" (Psalm 18:20).

"Take the Kingdom" Verses

"And from the days of John the Baptist until now the **kingdom** of heaven **suffers** violence, and the violent take it by force" (Matthew 11:12).

"Those great beasts, which are four, are four kings which arise out of the earth. But the saints of the Most High shall receive the kingdom, and possess the kingdom forever, even forever and ever" (Daniel 7:17-18).

"Jesus answered and said to him, 'Most assuredly, I say to you, unless one is **born again**, he cannot **see** the **kingdom** of God'" (John 3:3).

"But if I cast out demons by the Spirit of God, surely the kingdom of God has come upon you" (Matthew 12:28).

"Then the King will say to those on His right hand, 'Come, you blessed of My Father, inherit the kingdom prepared for you from the foundation of the world: for I was hungry and you gave Me food; I was thirsty and you gave Me drink; I was a stranger and you took Me in; I was naked and you clothed Me; I was sick and you visited Me; I was in prison and you came to Me.' ... And the King will answer and say to them, 'Assuredly, I say to you, inasmuch as you did it to one of the least of these My brethren, you did it to Me'" (Matthew 25:34-36,40).

"'Let the little children come to Me, and do not forbid them; for of such is the kingdom of God. Assuredly, I say to you, whoever does not receive the kingdom of God as a little child will by no means enter it'" (Mark 10:14-15).

"And heal the sick there, and say to them, 'The **kingdom** of God has **come** near to you'" (Luke 10:9).

"Whatever city you enter, and they receive you, eat such things as are set before you. And heal the sick there, and say to them, 'The kingdom of God has come near to you.' But whatever city you enter, and they do not receive you, go out into its streets and say, 'The very dust of your city which clings to us we wipe off against you. Nevertheless know this, that the kingdom of God has come near you.' But I say to you that it will be more tolerable in that Day for Sodom than for that city" (Luke 10:8-12).

"But if I cast out demons with the finger of God, surely the **kingdom** of God has **come** upon you" (Luke11:20).

"Then He took the cup, and gave thanks, and said, 'Take this and divide it among yourselves; for I say to you, I will not drink of the fruit of the vine until the kingdom of God comes'" (Luke 22:17-18).

"And He said to them, 'The kings of the Gentiles exercise lordship over them, and those who exercise authority over them are called "benefactors." But not so among you; on the contrary, he who is greatest among you, let him be as the younger, and he who governs as he who serves. For who is greater, he who sits at the table, or he who serves? Is it not he who sits at the table? Yet I am among you as the One who serves.

"'But you are those who have continued with Me in My trials. And I bestow upon you a kingdom, just as My Father bestowed one upon Me, that you may eat and drink at My table in My kingdom, and sit on thrones judging the twelve tribes of Israel'" (Luke 22:25-30).

"Then I heard a loud voice saying in heaven, 'Now salvation, and strength, and the **kingdom** of our

God, and the power of His Christ have **come**, for the accuser of our brethren, who accused them before our God day and night, has been cast down'" (Revelation 12:10).

"Our Father in heaven,
Hallowed be Your name.
Your kingdom come.
Your will be done
On earth as it is in heaven.
Give us day by day our daily bread.
And forgive us our sins,
For we also forgive everyone who is indebted to us.
And do not lead us into temptation,
But deliver us from the evil one" (Luke 11:2-4).

Rebuking Fear

Lord, I ask Your forgiveness for every fear in my life. I recognise that fear is also a lack of trust in You, so forgive me for not putting my trust in You. I choose to trust You. Sanctify me and show me Your love.

"There is no fear in love; but perfect love casts out fear, because fear involves torment. But he who fears has not been made perfect in love" (1 John 4:18).

God, You have not given me a spirit of fear, but a spirit of power, love and of a sound mind. With that knowledge I command my thoughts to be in captivity to the obedience of Christ (see 2 Timothy 1:7; 2 Corinthians 10:5).

I also know that if I need to speak, You will give me the words to speak because the Holy Spirit will teach me in that very hour what I ought to say (see Luke 12:12).

"[I] shall not be afraid of the terror by night, nor of the arrow that flies by day, nor of the pestilence that walks in darkness, nor of the destruction that lays waste at noonday. A thousand may fall at [my] side, and ten thousand at [my] right hand; but it shall not come near [me]" (Psalm 91:5-7).

"[If] I walk through the valley of the shadow of death, I will fear no evil; for You are with me; Your rod and Your staff, they comfort me. You prepare a table before me in the presence of my enemies; You anoint my head with oil; my cup runs over" (Psalm 23:4-5).

Lord I believe in You, and You say in Your Word: "Most assuredly, I say to you, he who believes in Me, the works that I do he will do also; and greater works than these he will do, because I go to My Father. And whatever you ask in My name, that I will do, that the Father may be glorified in the Son. If you ask anything in My name, I will do it" (John 14:12-14).

So, in the name of Jesus, I renounce and rebuke fear. "[Father, You] raised [Christ] from the dead and seated Him at [Your] right hand in the heavenly places, far above all principality and power and might and dominion, and every name that is named, not only in this age but also in that which is to come. And [You] put all things under His feet, and gave Him to be head over all things to the church, which is His body, the fullness of Him who fills all in all" (Ephesians 1:19-22).

Thank You, Lord, that You have disarmed principalities and powers. You have made a public spectacle of them, triumphing over them in it (see Colossians 2:15 & Psalm 91).

TRUE IDENTITY

As a child of God, I am a debtor, but not of the flesh, and I will not live according to the flesh, because if I live according to the flesh I will die; but if by the Spirit of God I put to death the deeds of the body, I will live (see Romans 8:12-13).

So, Father, I ask Your forgiveness for every deed of the flesh in my life. Please reveal those deeds to me, so that I can turn away from them. (Ask forgiveness for everything the Father shows you.)

I give up those deeds to You now in the name of Jesus. (You can name them when you give them up). I ask Your forgiveness for every time I have cursed my body, spirit, or soul. I renounce all those curses and break their power in my life now, in the name of Jesus. I forgive any person that has pronounced any curse against my body, soul, and spirit. I break also the power of those curses in my life now, in the name of Jesus. I choose to love myself because, Father, You love me. My body is the temple of the living God (see 1 Corinthians 3:16).

I declare that I am a son/daughter of God, led by the Spirit of God. "[I] did not receive the spirit of bondage again to fear, but [I] received the Spirit of adoption by whom [I] cry out, 'Abba, Father.' The Spirit Himself bears witness with [my] spirit that [I am a child] of God, and if [a child], then heir of God and joint heir with Christ, if indeed [I] suffer with Him, that [I] may also be glorified with Him" (Romans 8:14-17).

I am a member of "a chosen generation, a royal priesthood, a holy nation, His own special people, that [I] may proclaim the praises of Him who called [us] out of darkness into His marvellous light" (1 Peter 2:9).

Rebuking Shame
& Condemnation

Lord, I ask Your forgiveness for my sins and also for the shame and condemnation in my life. I choose to forgive myself for my mistakes and my sins.

Confess to God the reasons that put you into shame. Ask Him if there is someone you need to forgive.

I declare that "When [I was] dead in [my] sins and in the uncircumcision of [my] flesh, God made [me] alive with Christ. He forgave [me] all [my] sins, having cancelled the charge of [my] legal indebtedness, which stood against [me] and condemned [me]; he has taken it away, nailing it to the cross. And having disarmed the powers and authorities, he made a public spectacle of them, triumphing over them by the cross" (Colossians 2:13-15 NIV).

Lord, purify me now from all unrighteousness, according to Your Word in 1 John 1:9 (NIV) that says,

"If we confess our sins, he is faithful and just and will forgive us our sins and purify us from all unrighteousness."

I renounce and rebuke all shame and condemnation now, in the name of Jesus. "There is now no condemnation for [me because I am] in Christ Jesus, [and] through Christ Jesus the law of the Spirit who gives life has set [me] free from the law of sin and death" (Romans 8:1-2 NIV).

Your Word says, "The weapons of our warfare are not carnal but mighty in God for pulling down strongholds, casting down arguments and every high thing that exalts itself against the knowledge of God." Knowing that, I command my thoughts to be brought into captivity to the obedience of Christ (see 2 Corinthians 10:4-5).

"We know that whoever is born of God does not sin; but he who has been born of God keeps himself, and the wicked one does not touch him" (1 John 5:18).

"Now when they bring you to the synagogues and magistrates and authorities, do not worry about how or what you should answer, or what you should say. For the Holy Spirit will teach you in that very hour what you ought to say" (Luke 12:11-12).

If you still feel condemnation, you can soak and let God teach you if there is more to be done by confessing and forgiving any situation of your past that has not been dealt with, which God brings back to your mind. Also ask God to cleanse your thoughts.

Proclamation to Purify
the Mouth & Tongue

Lord, I ask Your forgiveness for every time I have used my tongue to curse, complain, or criticize. I break the power of those curses, complaints, and criticisms in my life and in the lives of those who have been negatively touched by them. Lord, purify my lips and heal my lips, mouth, and tongue; touch them with your live coal so that every word I have spoken may cause good and not harm (see Isaiah 6:6-7).

I bless my mouth in the name of Jesus, and I declare that my mouth is a well of life filled with love. I declare that wisdom is found on my lips because You, Lord, give me understanding. My mouth stores up knowledge because I am wise through Jesus. I choose to restrain my lips and be careful of the words that will come out of them. I choose righteousness, my tongue brings forth silver, and my lips feed many by the Word of God. My mouth brings forth wisdom and my lips know what is acceptable (see Proverbs 10:11-14, 19-21, 31-32).

I will be satisfied with good by the fruit of my mouth, and the recompense of my hands will be rendered to me. I choose to speak truth and declare righteousness, and my tongue will promote health because God gives me wisdom. My lips will be truthful and they shall be established forever (see Proverbs 12:6,14, 17-19).

My tongue will use knowledge rightly, and my tongue is a tree of life. My heart teaches my mouth and adds learning to my lips (see Proverbs 15:2,4; 16:23).

"[I] open my mouth with wisdom, and on [my] tongue is the law of kindness" (Proverbs 31:26).

"[My] stomach shall be satisfied from the fruit of [my] mouth; from the produce of [my] lips [I] shall be filled. [I will proclaim life with my tongue, because] death and life are in the power of the tongue, and those who love it will eat its fruit" (Proverbs 18:20-21).

More Verses to Purify
the Mouth & Tongue

"I will speak of excellent things, and from the opening of my lips will come right things; for my mouth will speak truth; wickedness is an abomination to my lips. All the words of my mouth are with righteousness; nothing crooked or perverse is in them" (Proverbs 8:6-8).

"There is gold and a multitude of rubies, but the lips of knowledge are a precious jewel" (Proverbs 20:15).

"Whoever guards his mouth and tongue keeps his soul from troubles" (Proverbs 21:23).

"[Lord,] You have tested my heart; You have visited me in the night; You have tried me and have found nothing; I have purposed that my mouth shall not transgress. Concerning the works of men, by the word of Your lips, I have kept away from the paths of the destroyer" (Psalm 17:3-4).

"I will bless the Lord at all times; His praise shall continually be in my mouth" (Psalm 34:1).

"The mouth of the righteous speaks wisdom, and his tongue talks of justice. The law of his God is in his heart; none of his steps shall slide" (Psalm 37:30-31).

"I said, 'I will guard my ways, lest I sin with my tongue; I will restrain my mouth with a muzzle, while the wicked are before me'" (Psalm 39:1).

"I have proclaimed the good news of righteousness in the great assembly; indeed, I do not restrain my lips, O Lord, You Yourself know" (Psalm 40:9).

"Because Your lovingkindness is better than life, my lips shall praise You. Thus I will bless You while I live; I will lift up my hands in Your name. My soul shall be satisfied as with marrow and fatness, and my mouth shall praise You with joyful lips. When I remember You on my bed, I meditate on You in the night watches" (Psalm 63:3-6).

"Let my prayer be set before You as incense, the lifting up of my hands as the evening sacrifice. Set a guard, O Lord, over my mouth; keep watch over the door of my lips" (Psalm 141:2-3).

"Let no corrupt word proceed out of your mouth, but what is good for necessary edification, that it may impart grace to the hearers" (Ephesians 4:29).

"How can you, being evil, speak good things? For out of the abundance of the heart the mouth speaks. A good man out of the good treasure of his heart brings forth good things, and an evil man out of the evil treasure brings forth evil things" (Matthew 12:34-35).

"But what does it say? 'The word is near you, in your mouth and in your heart' (that is, the word of faith which we preach): that if you confess with your mouth the Lord Jesus and believe in your heart that God has raised Him from the dead, you will be saved. For with the heart one believes unto righteousness, and with the mouth confession is made unto salvation" (Romans 10:8-10).

"Even so the tongue is a little member and boasts great things. See how great a forest a little fire kindles! ... Out of the same mouth proceed blessing and cursing. My brethren, these things ought not to be so. Does a spring send forth fresh water and bitter from the same opening? Can a fig tree, my brethren, bear olives, or a grapevine bear figs? Thus no spring yields both salt water and fresh" (James 3:5, 10-12).

Go from Rebellion
to Devotion

Lord, I ask Your forgiveness for any form of rebellion in my life. I have been in rebellion toward You and toward the authority You placed in my life. I have been in rebellion toward my parents and also toward injustice and life itself. Please forgive me.

Even if I don't always feel it, I know that You promise that no temptation will overtake me except such as is common to man; but God, You are faithful. You will not allow me to be tempted beyond what I am able, but with the temptation, You will also make the way of escape that I may be able to bear it (see 1 Corinthians 10:12-14). Show me Your way and the escape that You have provided for me. Thank You for the escape; thank You that You take good care of me. You will give me the strength to stand firm and follow Your ways.

"Create in me a clean heart, O God, and renew a steadfast spirit within me. Do not cast me away from Your presence, and do not take Your Holy Spirit from me. Restore to me the joy of Your salvation, and uphold me by Your generous Spirit. Then I will teach transgressors Your ways, and sinners shall be converted to You" (Psalm 51:10-13).

"Rejoice always, pray without ceasing, in everything give thanks; for this is the will of God in Christ Jesus for you. Do not quench the Spirit. Do not despise prophecies. Test all things; hold fast what is good. Abstain from every form of evil" (1 Thessalonians 5:16-22).

Ask for Wisdom

Lord, I ask Your forgiveness for not seeking You and obeying Your Word, for not seeking Your Kingdom first. I want my ways to be right and I want to obey Your command.

I choose to be righteous, so I will study how to answer, and I trust that You will teach me (see Proverbs 15:28).

I will prepare my heart by forgiveness and by singing hymns and psalms to You. I believe You will answer with Your tongue to bless my life and also You will confound the enemy who comes against me, O Lord. Weigh my spirit and teach me how to commit my works to You so that my thoughts will be established. Direct my steps in Your way (see Proverbs 16:1-3, 9)

I choose to be a prudent man/women; my heart is acquiring knowledge, and as a wise person, my ear seeks knowledge (see Proverbs 18:15).

"Teach me Your way, O Lord; I will walk in Your truth; unite my heart to fear Your name. I will praise You, O Lord my God, with all my heart, and I will glorify Your name forevermore. For great is Your mercy toward me, and You have delivered my soul from the depths of Sheol" (Psalm 86:11-13).

Lord, I receive your words and I treasure your commands within me. I incline my ear to wisdom and apply my heart to understanding. Yes, I cry out for discernment, and I lift up my voice for understanding. I seek her as silver and search for her as for hidden treasures because I want to understand the fear of the Lord and find the knowledge of God. Thank You, Lord, that You give wisdom; from Your mouth comes knowledge and understanding. You store up sound wisdom for the upright; You are a shield to those who walk uprightly. You guard the paths of justice, and preserve my way. I will understand righteousness and justice, equity, and every good path (see Proverbs 2:2-9).

Prayer Against Injustice

Father, I ask Your forgiveness for any judgement and bitterness I have in my heart toward _____.

Name the person If the injustice comes from the enemy, ask if there is a door open in your life. If you have bitterness in your heart or if you are angry toward God, ask Him to forgive you, and ask if there is anything else in which you need to ask for God's forgiveness.

I forgive myself for all the mistakes I made in that situation. I trust in You and even in my mistakes I believe that You, O God, cause everything to work together for my good, because I love You, and I am called according to Your purpose for me (see Romans 8:28 NLT).

Lord, I trust in You and I choose to do good. I will dwell in the land and feed on Your faithfulness. I will delight myself in You, Lord, and You shall give me the desires of my heart. I choose to commit my way to You, Lord, to trust also in You, and You shall bring it to pass. You shall bring forth my righteousness as the light and my justice as the noonday (see Psalm 37:3-6).

My mouth will speak wisdom and my tongue talks of justice. The law of my God is in my heart; none of my steps shall slide (see Psalm 37:30-31).

"Lead me, O Lord, in Your righteousness because of my enemies; make Your way straight before my face" (Psalm 5:8).

I believe that even if they bring me to the synagogues, magistrates, and authorities, I do not need to worry about how or what I should answer or what I should say. For the Holy Spirit will teach me in that very hour what I ought to say (see Luke 12:11-12).

Part 4:

Healing Prayer
with Biblical Declaration

Notes on Healing

For healing, I have separated the healing needs by category and body parts. Sickness and pain problems may come from many areas in our lives, like sin or fear – sometimes from us or from our ancestors. Sickness can also come from curses and witchcraft, or simply from the enemy who tries to destroy us.

You may begin by declaring the general prayer for sickness to build your faith. To be more specific, there are declarations by category and part, matching the kind of sins that can bring a specific sickness, infirmity, or disease together with a prayer of forgiveness. If you don't have a specific sin in your life, skip it and go to the next part. The act of breaking curses pronounced against you – asking forgiveness and breaking the generational curses – is always good; you don't know what you carry from your family or what has been said against you. Don't forget, if you have relatives still alive that could contribute to the curses, you may have to do this again occassionally.

General Healing

If this is the first time you pray this prayer, please read the notes on healing (p. 119).

"[Jesus] himself bore our sins in his body on the cross, so that we might die to sins and live for righteousness; 'by his wounds you have been healed'" (1 Peter 2:24 NIV).

Lord I confess that I am a sinner, and I ask Your forgiveness for all my sins. I ask Your forgiveness for every time I complained about my situation and every time I have cursed myself. I forgive any person that has spoken against my healing or cursed me by their words, whether they are known by me or not. I break every curse now, in the name of Jesus, that I have pronounced against myself or someone else has pronounced against me. If there are specific sins that You want me to confess, which keep me from having the victory in my healing, I pray that You will reveal those to me. (Confess anything that comes to your mind that has not been confessed in the past.)

I ask Your forgiveness for every time I forgot Your law and believed my circumstances instead of Your Word. I choose to believe Your Word and declare it. "My son, do not forget my law, but let your heart keep my commands; for length of days and long life and peace they will add to you" (Proverbs 3:1-2).

According to 1 Peter 2:24, Jesus not only died for my sins but also for my healing. It is done, so I renounce now all sickness, all disease, all infirmity, all physical pain, all lies of the enemy over my body, all dysfunction in my body, and all curses. I break your power over my body! Now you have no more legal right over my life because "God made [me] alive with Christ. He forgave [me] all [my] sins, having cancelled the charge of [my] legal indebtedness, which stood against [me] and condemned [me]; he has taken it away, nailing it to the cross. [Jesus has] disarmed the powers and authorities, he made a public spectacle of them, triumphing over them by the cross" (Colossians 2:13-15 NIV).

I will serve the Lord my God, and He will bless my bread and my water. And He will take sickness away from me. I shall not suffer miscarriage or be barren in my land, and I will fulfil the number of my days (see Exodus 23:25-26). So, I command my digestive system and my reproductive system to be made whole and healthy.

"Let them give thanks to the Lord for his unfailing love and his wonderful deeds for mankind, for he satisfies the thirsty and fills the hungry with good things" (Psalm 107:8-9 NIV).

I also ask forgiveness for all the sins of my parents and grandparents up to the tenth generation (see Daniel 9). I break every generational curse that has brought sickness, infirmity, physical pain, and dysfunction in my body. I bless my body. I have been created in God's image, so I command every part of my body to be made whole now, in the name of Jesus. Lord, my hope is in You, and I trust You to renew my strength.

"[I] will soar on wings like eagles; [I] will run and not grow weary, [I] will walk and not be faint" (Isaiah 40:31 NIV).

The Bones, Muscles, & Ligaments

(Articulation, back, neck, arms, knees, legs)

Lord, I ask Your forgiveness for my sins and iniquity (see Psalm 38:3; 31:10). Lord, I ask Your forgiveness for any form of shame, envy, jealousy, and bitterness in my life (see Proverbs 12:4; 14:30). I ask Your forgiveness for every time I have had shame of You, Your Word or my belief in You, and every time I did not stand for the truth (see Psalm 32:3). I also ask Your forgiveness for all the times I did not put my trust in You in my situation. Forgive me for my pride (see Proverbs 3:7-8; 17:22; & Psalm 32:3). Now, in the name of Jesus, I renounce all kind of infirmity in my body. I command my bones to be healthy and all the articulation in my body to be made whole. I command my vertebrae to be aligned and in God's order. I command my ligaments, cartilage, and muscles to strengthen and be aligned as God created them to be.

I command the pain and lies of the enemy to leave now, in the name of Jesus.

I will rejoice myself in the Lord because He is the One who makes my bones healthy (see Proverbs 15:30; 17:22).

"Therefore all those who devour [me] shall be devoured; and all [my] adversaries, every one of them, shall go into captivity; those who plunder [me] shall become plunder, and all who prey upon [me] [God] will make a prey. For [God] will restore health to [me] and heal [me] of my wounds" (Jeremiah 30:16-17).

I choose to fear the Lord and depart from evil. It will be health to my flesh and strength to my bones (see Proverbs 3:7-8).

Even if I have many afflictions, God will deliver me from them all and, because I am righteous through the blood of Jesus, He will guard all my bones and none of them will be broken (see Psalm 34:19-20).

The Head

Lord, I ask Your forgiveness for every time I have lacked love. I ask Your forgiveness for not loving You with all my heart, all my soul, all my strength, and all my mind. Sometimes I put other things or people before You; please forgive me. I ask Your forgiveness for not loving myself and not loving my neighbour, friend, and family like Jesus. I choose to love You with all my heart, with all my soul, with all my strength, and with all my mind, so please increase my love for You and give me discernment so that I will make good choices for You. I choose to love myself because You have created me, and I am wonderfully made. I choose to love my neighbours, friends, and family as I love myself (see Luke 10:27).

I ask Your forgiveness for my fears and worries, Lord. I come to You and choose to give You my heavy load so that You will give me rest. I choose to take Your yoke instead and learn from You, because You are gentle and lowly in heart, and I will find rest for my soul. I take Your yoke that is easy and Your burden, which is light (see Matthew 11:28-30).

I choose to be righteous and to seek righteousness, because blessings are on the head of the righteous, and the memory of the righteous is blessed (see Proverbs 10:6-7).

I ask Your forgiveness for every time I lack wisdom or do not walk in wisdom. Therefore, I choose to get wisdom. Lord, teach me Your way through Your Word, and I will get understanding. I know that if I exalt wisdom she will promote me; she will bring me honour, so I choose to embrace her. And she will place on my head an ornament of grace; a crown of glory she will deliver to me (see Proverbs 4:7-9).

Lord I know that "The weapons of our warfare are not carnal but mighty in God for pulling down strongholds, casting down arguments and every high thing that exalts itself against the knowledge of God, bringing every thought into captivity to the obedience of Christ, and being ready to punish all disobedience when your obedience is fulfilled" (2 Corinthians 10:4-6).

Knowing that, I choose to meditate on things that are true, things that are noble, things that are just, things that are pure, things that are lovely, and things that are of good report to see if there is any virtue and anything praiseworthy. The things I learned, received, heard, and saw in the gospel, these I will do, and the God of peace will be with me (see Philippians 4:8-9).

More Verses for the Head

"But You, O Lord, are a shield for me, my glory and the One who lifts up my head. I cried to the Lord with my voice, and He heard me from His holy hill. Selah. I lay down and slept; I awoke, for the Lord sustained me. I will not be afraid of ten thousands of people who have set themselves against me all around" (Psalm 3:3-6).

"Yea, though I walk through the valley of the shadow of death, I will fear no evil; for You are with me; your rod and Your staff, they comfort me. You prepare a table before me in the presence of my enemies; you anoint my head with oil" (Psalm 23:4-5).

"I said to the Lord: 'You are my God; hear the voice of my supplications, O Lord. O God the Lord, the strength of my salvation, You have covered my head in the day of battle'" (Psalm 140:6-7).

"But You, O Lord, are a shield for me, my glory and the One who lifts up my head" (Psalm 3:3).

"One thing I have desired of the Lord, that will I seek: that I may dwell in the house of the Lord all the days of my life, to behold the beauty of the Lord, and to inquire in His temple. For in the time of trouble He shall hide me in His pavilion; in the secret place of His tabernacle he shall hide me; He shall set me high upon a rock. And now my head shall be lifted up above my enemies all around me; therefore I will offer sacrifices of joy in His tabernacle; I will sing, yes, I will sing praises to the Lord" (Psalm 27:4-6).

The Heart

"Above all else, guard your heart, for everything you do flows from it" (Proverbs 4:23 NIV). Lord, I confess that I have not guarded my heart above all else, and I ask Your forgiveness for it.

I ask Your forgiveness for envy and covetousness; I choose to be zealous for the fear of God (see Proverbs 23:17).

I also ask Your forgiveness for any form of perversity in my life, because it is written in Proverbs that perversity is in the heart (see Proverbs 6:14). Search my heart, O Lord, and reveal to me any perverse thoughts or mindsets so that I will turn away from them and be Your delight (see Proverbs 11:20). I ask Your forgiveness for every time my heart has backslidden, and I declare that I am a good man/woman, and I will be satisfied in You (see Proverbs 14:14).

I ask Your forgiveness for any bitterness in my heart (see Proverbs 14:10).

Ask God if there is someone you need to forgive, and forgive them.

I ask Your forgiveness for every time I have acted impulsively or foolishly instead of wisely. I declare that I am a prudent man/woman, and I bless my heartbeat (see Proverbs 12:23; 14:33).

Lord I put my hope in You and my desires in You. Sanctified, my hope and desires will be a tree of life (see Proverbs 13:12).

Lord, help my heart to retain Your Word, so that I can keep Your commands and live (see Proverbs 4:4).

Wisdom is entering my heart, and knowledge is pleasant to my soul. Lord, teach me how to be discreet and have understanding so that I can stay far from the way of evil (see Proverbs 2:10-12).

I command my heart to be made whole and to function upon God's order. Lord, I wait on You; I am of good courage and, as in Psalm 27:14, You shall strengthen my heart. You create in me a pure heart, O God, and You renew a steadfast spirit within me (see Psalm 51:10 NIV).

"My son, keep your father's command, and do not forsake the law of your mother. Bind them continually upon your heart; tie them around your neck. When you roam, they will lead you; when you sleep, they will keep you; and when you awake, they will speak with you. For the commandment is a lamp, and the law a light; reproofs of instruction are the way of life" (Proverbs 6:20-23).

"He who loves purity of heart and has grace on his lips, the king will be his friend" (Proverbs 22:11).

"The humble shall see this and be glad; and you who seek God, your hearts shall live" (Psalm 69:32).

"I will give them an undivided heart and put a new spirit in them; I will remove from them their heart of stone and give them a heart of flesh" (Ezekiel 11:19 NIV).

THE FIVE SENSES

The five senses are also five doors the enemy uses to come into your life. It is important to keep them clean and be careful of what you let enter by those doors. Sometimes we go into places, hear things we would not listen to at home, or see things we would not look at otherwise. In our family, we call it spiritual pollution, and we ask Jesus to cleanse us with His blood from all spiritual pollution we have been in.

"Be sober, be vigilant; because your adversary the devil walks about like a roaring lion, seeking whom he may devour. Resist him, steadfast in the faith, knowing that the same sufferings are experienced by your brotherhood in the world" (1 Peter 5:8-9).

The Eyes

Lord, I ask Your forgiveness for every time I have looked at or watched things unclean. I also ask Your forgiveness for every time I have closed my eyes instead of looking at what my loved one wanted to show me, or seeing the suffering around me. I break every curse of blindness, pain, presbyopia, myopia, astigmatism, glaucoma, cataract, and malfunction over my eyes now, in the name of Jesus. I command my eyes to be made whole now and every part of my eyes to work properly according to God's order.

"Blessed are your eyes for they see, and your ears for they hear" (Matthew 13:16).

"Moses was one hundred and twenty years old when he died. His eyes were not dim nor his natural vigour diminished" (Deuteronomy 34:7).

THE EARS

Lord, I ask Your forgiveness for every time I have listened to the lies of the enemy instead of listening to You. I ask Your forgiveness for everything unclean that I have let enter through my ears. I ask Your forgiveness for every time I have closed my ears instead of listening to what my loved one had to say, and every time I closed my ears on what Your Word says. I break every curse of deafness, pain, tinnitus, and malfunction over my ears now, in the name of Jesus. I command my ears to be made whole now, and every part of my ears to work properly according to God's order. Lord, I pray that You give me discernment in what I listen to, so my ears will glorify You in my everyday life.

"Blessed are your eyes for they see, and your ears for they hear" (Matthew 13:16).

My ears hear the rebukes of life because I declare Your Word through my mouth so I will abide among the wise (see Proverbs 15:31).

THE NOSE

Lord, I ask Your forgiveness for any kind of anger and rage in my life (see Proverbs 30:33; 2 Kings 19:27-29).

I rebuke any cold or breathing allergy. I command my nose to be made whole so that I can breathe properly.

THE MOUTH

The mouth is one of the most important parts of the body when praying for healing and against curses. See the chapter, *Proclamation to Purify the Mouth and Tongue* (p.105).

MORE VERSES FOR HEALING

"Then I will give them one heart, and I will put a new spirit within them, and take the stony heart out of their flesh, and give them a heart of flesh, that they may walk in My statutes and keep My judgements and do them; and they shall be My people, and I will be their God" (Ezekiel 11:19-20).

"So you shall serve the Lord your God, and He will bless your bread and your water. And I will take sickness away from the midst of you. No one shall suffer miscarriage or be barren in your land; I will fulfil the number of your days" (Exodus 23:25-26).

"'Therefore all those who devour you shall be devoured; and all your adversaries, every one of them, shall go into captivity; those who plunder you shall become plunder, and all who prey upon you I will make a prey. For I will restore health to you and heal you of your wounds,' says the Lord, 'because they called you an outcast saying: "This is Zion; no one seeks her"'" (Jeremiah 30:16-17).

"Beloved, I pray that you may prosper in all things and be in health, just as your soul prospers. For I rejoiced greatly when brethren came and testified of the truth that is in you, just as you walk in the truth. I have no greater joy than to hear that my children walk in truth" (3 John 2-4).

"My son, give attention to my words; incline your ear to my sayings. Do not let them depart from your eyes; keep them in the midst of your heart; for they are life to those who find them, and health to all their flesh. Keep your heart with all diligence, for out of it spring the issues of life. Put away from you a deceitful mouth, and put perverse lips far from you. Let your eyes look straight ahead, and your eyelids look right before you. Ponder the path of your feet, and let all your ways be established. Do not turn to the right or the left; remove your foot from evil" (Proverbs 4:20-27).

"Bless the Lord, O my soul; and all that is within me, bless His holy name! Bless the Lord, O my soul, and forget not all His benefits: Who forgives all your iniquities, Who heals all your diseases, Who redeems your life from destruction, Who crowns you with loving kindness and tender mercies, Who satisfies your mouth with good things, so that your youth is renewed like the eagle's" (Psalm 103:1-5).

"It is the Spirit who gives life; the flesh profits nothing. The words that I speak to you are spirit, and they are life" (John 6:63).

"Come to Me, all you who labour and are heavy laden, and I will give you rest. Take My yoke upon you and learn from Me, for I am gentle and lowly in heart, and you will find rest for your souls. For My yoke is easy and My burden is light" (Matthew 11:28-30).

"And Jesus went about all Galilee, teaching in their synagogues, preaching the gospel of the kingdom, and healing all kinds of sickness and all kinds of disease among the people. Then His fame went throughout all Syria; and they brought to Him all sick people who were afflicted with various diseases and torments, and those who were demon-possessed, epileptics, and paralytics; and He healed them" (Matthew 4:23-24).

"For though we walk in the flesh, we do not war according to the flesh. For the weapons of our warfare are not carnal but mighty in God for pulling down strongholds, casting down arguments and every high thing that exalts itself against the knowledge of God, bringing every thought into captivity to the obedience of Christ, and being ready to punish all disobedience when your obedience is fulfilled" (2 Corinthians 10:3-6).

About the Author

Genevieve Roy and her husband Robert are from Quebec. They met in the midst of a powerful move of the Holy Spirit and wed in 1995; they now have four children. The Roys have seen many miracles, healings, and victories in their home. They have taught the prophetic for many years and are actively involved in intercession for their church, city, and on different occasion for Canada and Israel. They have been part of different inner healing ministries and they actually do ministries with the SOZO team of British Columbia.

Genevieve is gifted in prophetic dance, flagging and painting. She is one of the prophetic voices for her local church and she also has a sharp discernment. She is a prayer warrior and likes to do prophetic intercession and declaration of the word of God.

For more information go to:
www.swordofwisdom.ca